T0132456

Windows of Heaven Pouring Out Blessings

Scriptures: King James Version
Book Cover Designed By:
Viccardo Brown (grandson)
(Vardo)

Author: Louise T. Coleman
(Neaice)

WestBow Press books may be ordered through booksellers or by contacting:

WestBow Press
A Division of Thomas Nelson & Zondervan
1663 Liberty Drive
Bloomington, IN 47403
www.westbowpress.com
844-714-3454

Book Cover Design by: Viccardo Brown

Scripture quotations are taken from King James version of the Bible, public domain.

ISBN: 979-8-3850-0118-7 (sc)
ISBN: 979-8-3850-0119-4 (e)

Library of Congress Control Number: 2023911285

Print information available on the last page.

WestBow Press rev. date: 09/15/2023

Contents

Preface

Because he is God: he took matters into his hands.

He spoke into existence light and divided the light from the darkness and created the heaven and earth.

The first book of the bible, Genesis is an affirmation that begins with the fact of creation.

This book builds a unique picture of life and death, sin and redemption, good over evil in God's eternal kingdom.

Sin and disobedience distorted God's original plan for mankind. His, intention were and are blessings for his children on this earthly kingdom.

My goal is to teach sound doctrine according to the word of God.

This doctrine will guide your life, increase your faith, and you will know for yourself that God is real: and his word is true.

He is in the blessing business.

WINDOWS OF HEAVEN
POURING OUT BLESSINGS

Introduction

Windows of Heaven

Pouring

Out

Blessings

Malachi 3:10

Bring ye all the tithes into the storehouse, that there may be meat in mine house, and prove me now herewith, saith the Lord of hosts, if I will not open you the windows of heaven, and pour you out a blessing, that there shall not be room enough to receive it.

From The Authors Desk

I am the founder of Memoirs of a Christians Life Ministry. This is my third book written under the anointing of the Holy Spirit, teaching: personal responsibility blended with obedience and spiritual growth.

In my wildest dream I never thought at this stage in my life I would be putting God's word in print for others to read. The responses have been so great that I am encouraged to continue to write, lifting up the name of Jesus.

Book #1: Memoirs of a Christian Life- 2016
Book #2: Who Is this man Jesus- 2019
Book #3: Windows of Heaven Pouring Out Blessings- 2023

Thank God for every one that has and will read my books. As per the testimonies (feedback) I have received; lives have been touched in a positive way.

Through my ministry the books are being read in twelve states (excluding Amazon, Barnes & Noble, E Books etc.)

Westbow Press is the publisher of 2016-2019 writings.

These are the states I have had a book signing, or mail orders.

Florida	Maryland	Alabama	Philadelphia
Mississippi	New Jersey	Georgia	New York
Carolina's	Ohio	Virginia	California

I am counting my blessings one by one because the books help support the ministry.

In closing position yourself, for the purpose of living and serving God; no matter what stage of life you are in.

Joshua 24:15
Choose ye this day whom you will serve.

JESUS IS THE BLESSER

Jesus Is The Blesser

The Church Is
The Storehouse

Malachi 3:10
Bring Ye all the Tithes into the
storehouse, that there may be meat in
mine house, and prove me now herewith,
saith the lord of hosts, If I will not
open you the windows of heaven, and
pour you out a blessing, that there
shall not be room enough to receive it.

Members

Widows

Families

Children

Help the
poor and needy

Song	You Can't Beat God's Giving
Written by	Doris Akers

This song is inspiring and uplifting, It makes you inhale and exhale, because you realize how great God is.

It is written in all types of Hymn books in different languages.

Sunday Morning   This song is a staple in the Christian Church.

First Stanza   You can't beat God's giving, no matter how hard you try and just as sure as you are living, and the Lord is in Heaven on high.
The more you give, the more he gives to you but keep on giving because its really true that you can't beat God's giving no matter how you try.

If you really want to be encouraged and blessed listen to the late (Billy Preston) you can't beat God's giving-Official video on you tube.

This song answers the question: There is no competition between God and man, he wins.

BLESSINGS UNFOLDING
MALACHI 3:10

Apostle Paul's Personal Letters

Apostle Paul's Letter

Blessings Unfolding

We are in the process of understanding how to make it over in Jesus name.

Advancing The Gospel

Apostle Paul has made it over following Christ: encouraging his fellow labours to see the blessing in his imprisonment.

The book of Philippians demonstrates how Paul found the Lord in a mighty way.

From a persecutor of the gospel of Jesus Christ, to a full pledge Christian willing to die for the cause of Christ.

Once he was converted there were four great convictions that ruled his life:
Jesus is Lord.
Jesus name must be preached.
I "am" God's instrument.
The gospel (Jesus Christ) is universal, including the gentiles.

Dead Or Alive

He adhered to the spirit of humility and obedience; the same as Christ did: because he wanted Christ to be magnified in his body whether it be by life or death.

Philippians 1:21

For to me to live in Christ, and to die is gain.

But if I live in the flesh, this is the fruit of my labour; yet what I shall choose I wot not.

Trust God

My flesh is weak, and I do not always make the right choice. (do you trust yourself?)

1

When you are feeling overwhelmed allow the Holy Spirit to continue a good work in your life, it will give you the strength to make the right choice.

Personal

When you reach a certain plateau in life (old age or sickness) when you are ready to die through it all God says when.

Philippians 1:23

For I am in a strait betwixt tow, having a desire to depart, and to be with Christ; which is far better:

Philippians

The highlight of these letters is in chapter two verse eight.

Philippians 2:8

And being found in fashion as a man, he humbled himself, and became obedient unto death, even the death of the cross. (Jesus)

The Son Jesus Christ

He did not worry about his reputation, a servant; he moved from spirit to flesh: humbled as a lamb, going about his fathers' business.

Prison

Paul is inspired to continue to work for the Lord under dye strait conditions because he was covered under the blood of the cross (Jesus is the cross).

Philippians 3:12

Not as though I had already attained, either were already perfect: but I follow after, if that I may apprehend that for which also I am apprehended of Christ Jesus.

Because he was still abiding in the flesh for our sake he did not murmur, fuss, or dispute (ref: Philippians 2:14) he humbled himself and continued to advance the gospel of Jesus Christ.

Humility is a virtue that puts you in a place of tranquility where peace, grace, and mercy will sustain you.

Together
Obedience is a lifestyle that requires practice.

Obedience and humility work hand and hand to gain the best results.

Public Announcement
Pauls' encounter at Damascus (Acts chapter nine) changed his name from Saul to Paul. This is a proclamation to the world.
When he calls you, he has a way of getting your attention (we are all called to righteousness).

Philippians 2:10
That at the name of Jesus every knee should bow, of things in heaven, and things in earth, and things under the earth;

Philippians 2:11
And that every tongue should confess that Jesus Christ is Lord, to the glory of God the Father. (Confirmation: Romans 14:11)

Philippians 2:12
Wherefore, my beloved, as ye have always obeyed, not as in my presence only, but now much more in my absence, work out your own salvation with fear and trembling.

Philippians 4:9
Those things, which ye have both learned and received, and heard, and seen in me, do: and the God of peace shall be with you.

Using Paul's criteria:
What goals are you committed to in your life?
Address the relationship you find hard to maintain.
What characterizes mature planning skills in your life?
Do you have the attitude of obedience and humility?
Do you put Godly living in practice?

Follow Apostle Pauls' example; and know that to obey is better than sacrifice and obedience opens the pathway to blessing.

Blessings increase your physical and mental health, which penetrates your demeanor and improves your character.

THE WEB OF RIGHTEOUSNESS

COVERED BY THE BLOOD
BLESSINGS PROMISED

L.T.

HEALING MIND

BODY & SOUL

PEACE

GRACE

FREEDOM FROM SIN

LOVE

OBEDIENCE

HAPPINESS

MERCY

KINGDOM

JESUS

HOLY

REDEMPTION

FORGIVENESS

HOLY SPIRIT

SALVATION

The Web Of Righteousness

John 7:38   He that believeth on me, as the scripture hath said, out of his belly shall flow rivers of living water.

Cross over to the web of righteousness and start life anew, the heavens open when one sinner repents.

Luke 15:7   I say unto you, that likewise joy shall be in heaven over one sinner that repenteth, more than over ninety and nine just persons, which need no repentance.

If you have repented of your sins, you are there. God is proud of you. He worries about the unsaved.

Matthew 18:11   For the Son of man is come to save that which was lost.

Luke 19:10   For the son of man is come to seek and to save that which was lost.

On The Cross   His sole purpose is that not one soul should be lost. Thank God you have been founded through his blood.

In this web you will find redemption, forgiveness and God will cloth you with the garment of righteousness: salvation is free.

The Holy Ghost   At this point you have survived the destruction, and endured the weeping, and mourning: Now you are ready to draw water from the well that is in you springing up into everlasting life.

This is the web of freedom, grace, and mercy abides, experiencing love, joy, peace, healing, and blessings overflowing.

You must repent and turn from your wicked ways in order to live in the web of righteousness and reap the benefits.

Luke 13:3

I tell you, Nay: but, except ye repent, ye shall all likewise perish.

Listen to the voice of the Lord, his word is his voice. Obedience is better than sacrifice. (See 1 Samuel 15:22)

If you are lost come home; Jesus is waiting for you. If you are saved stay the course and continue to grow in grace, he is holding you in the hollow of his hand.

Remember the Promise (See 2 Chronicles 7:14)

We Are His People

The Three "R's"

The Three "Rs" statements

Practice What You Preach

1. Do right.
2. Live righteously.
3. Be responsible.

Malachi 3:6-10

Hindering Your Blessings

Let us answer the question: will a man rob God?

Money is not the main issue in this chapter, yet it is important for the purpose of maintaining and running God's business. (The physical church).

Property, utilities, repairs, community services as the leadership sees fit according to God's word, following the by-laws.

Trust And Obey

Malachi: is speaking about full commitment during the time of struggles and poverty.

It is not always easy to support the church financially, but you must be committed to the cause.

Pay Your Tithes And Free Will Offerings

How strong is your faith? Do you truly trust him for all your needs?

Government

Just as Caesar takes his assessment off the top at the highest rate, God ask for less (10%-free will offerings is your choice).

In verse six, God makes a profound statement to get your attention; and make sure you understand if there is fault, it is you not him.

Malachi 3:6

For I am the Lord, I change not.

Believe

Trust me and obey; and receive the promised increase for you and your household.

Hope And A Future

What he said he would do for you he will do, he is a promise keeper, with unconditional love he wants you to prosper.

Jeremiah 29:11

For I know the thoughts that I think toward you, saith the Lord, thoughts of peace, and not of evil, to give you an expected end.

The question: Will a man Rob God? YES HE WILL

Man has robbed God and themselves through:

Relationship (with God and man)
Unfaithfulness
Disobedience
No brotherly love

Malachi 3:7

Even from the days of your fathers ye are gone away from mine ordinances and have not kept them. Return unto me, and I will return unto you, saith the Lord of hosts. But ye said, wherein shall we return.

Bewildered

Stop questioning the statement: face the truth, we are not always on target. Living in denial is not good. Remember nobody is perfect but Jesus.

Lost You Way

When heaven seems silent and still your relationship with him seems unreal, you are experiencing drifting faith leaving you unable to count your blessings.

The Kings Of Kings

Be strong and reflect on what he has done, know who you are serving. How many times has he came through for you?

Confirmation Scriptures:

Proverbs 3:9

Honour the Lord with thy substance, and with the firstfruits of all thine increase.

Proverbs 3:10

So shall thy barns be filled with plenty, and thy presses shall burst out with new wine.

The proverbs of King Solomon: The wisest king that ever lived, full of wisdom, knowledge and understanding gave insight on the topic of giving.

Proverbs the 20th book of the bible.
Malachi the 39th book of the bible.
Both books are found in the Old Testament

THE WEB OF CORRUPTION
BLESSING BLOCKERS   PROGRESS STOPPERS

STUBBORNESS

UNFORG...N

DISOBEDIENCE

SELFISHNESS

SHAME

DRU...

PILLS

OPIOD EPIDEMIC

MARIJAUNA

DESTRUCTION

ADULTERY

STRIFE

MEAN-SPIRIT

DISEASE

SUFFERING

HATRED

TOBACCO

ALCOHOL

SORROW

PORNOGRAPHY

The Web Of Corruption

Joshua 24:15
And if it seem evil unto you to serve the Lord, choose you this day whom ye will serve; whether the gods which your fathers served that were on the other side of the flood, or the gods of the Amorites, in whose land ye dwell: but as for me and my house we will serve the Lord.

Renewed Covenant
This is Joshua's fair well message to Israel and the new generation; he is nearly a hundred and ten years old (110) and he made a choice to follow Jesus.

Righteousness Or Corruption
It is your choice: God is so good he allows you to make the choice (right or wrong). However, as a rule we make the wrong choice.

Corruption
This web continues to destroy millions of lives around the world.

The Web
How many people are alive but are just existing, caught in the web?

Crafty
The web of corruption is a trap spun by sin, put together in a careful complicated way making it hard for you to break the threads.

Vegetated State
This web tangles you up: taking away your dignity and respect, sucking the life out of you short circuiting your brain creating doubt, fear, weakness, and shame.

Corruption affects the mind, body, and soul.
Mind- causes mental illness and instability.

The Temple Of God

Body- sickness and diseases that cripples the youth and weakens the old.

Soul- your soul belongs to God; the inner spirit is disconnected from the son (Jesus Christ).

Come To Jesus

You do not have to live in a vulnerable state; repent of your sins and let Jesus take over. He will cure your sickness and heal your broken heart.

Hebrews 12:1

Wherefore seeing we also are compassed about with so great a cloud of witnesses, let us lay aside every weight, and the sin which doth so easily beset us, and let us run with patience the race that is set before us,

Repentance Is The Key

Nothing is impossible with God, He knows the flesh is weak (we make mistakes) however, forgiveness, grace, and mercy is available just for the asking.

Corruption has a strong hold on society because we do not root up/root out the source of the problem. If you need help to break the threads call on Jesus, he will answer your prayer.

Final Note

Before you make the decision to join the web of corruption, apply logic use your sense of reasoning.

Understanding

Interpretation- Read the instructions before you start the project (count up the cost).

Choose Right Not Wrong

Application- make sure you have the right tools for the job.

Life/ Death

Observation- survey your surroundings for pitfalls; how much are you willing to pay.

Blessings In Disguise

BLESSINGS IN DISGUISE

Blessings In The Mist Of A Crisis

Blessings In Disguise

Apostle Paul speaks from his heart in the midst of a crisis writing from prison to the people who are concerned about his well- being.

Unbelievable

Against all odds (locked up in prison) he is talking about joy.
Joy in the gospel.
Joy in following Jesus.
Joy through commitment.
Joy in the Lord (Just to know him).

God presence means inner peace. Can you see the blessings?

Apostle Paul

His peace surpasses our understanding however, he understood that his name was written in the book of life and his present condition was just a test.

Philippians 4:6

Be careful for nothing; but in every thing by prayer and supplication with thanksgiving let your requests be made known unto God.

Philippians 4:7

And the peace of God, which passeth all understanding, shall keep your hearts and minds through Christ Jesus.

Trials And Tribulations

Are you grounded in Jesus? Just trust and obey his word. Keep the faith and your blessings will flow.

Stumbling

The four stumbling blocks that prevents your blessings, and puts a noose around your neck and robs you of your peace and happiness are:

Being	Irresponsible. Enabler. Procrastinator. Stubborn.
Irresponsible	No sense of duties, doing as you please having no consideration for others. Avoiding responsibilities.
Enabler	Take control, overstepping your boundaries using the word help. Are you a control freak? It must be my way or no way.
Procrastinator	I will get to it. When? Slow on the draw most of the time to late. You cannot go back. Life moves forward.
Stubbornness	Just because you can; allowing bad behavior to rule affording no satisfaction because you think you have the upper hand. You are not allowing the Holy Spirit to operate in you. (Do you have it)?
Sin	Remember the noose: it's funny the noose is pulled as tight as you can stand it before you drop like a sack of potatoes, then the question is, where am I?
Bad Deeds	You put the noose around your neck. How much has it cost you? Over a period of time, it does not matter the damage is done, now comes consequences and repercussions you will pay for your bad behavior.

Do not allow yourself to feel secure with bad behavior. Hearts and minds change when there is no hope.

If you are not willing to change; why cause pain and suffering move on and position yourself and others for a blessing.

Philippians 4:8

Finally, brethren, whatsoever things are true, whatsoever things are honest, whatsoever things are just, whatsoever things are pure, whatsoever things are lovely, whatsoever things are of good report; if there be any virtue, and if there be any praise, think on these things.

Highlight the word virtue and answer the following questions:
Do you have honor and respect?
Do you see other's needs?
Do you have a caring heart?

If so, follow Apostle Paul's example and receive your blessings as they unfold.

Blessings Flowing

Malachi 3:10

Promised

Pouring into
your life

Blessings Flow With Wisdom Knowledge And Understanding

The book of Proverbs is the dictionary that gives the correct definition for moral behavior, stating the importance of wisdom, knowledge and understanding.

Increasing your ability to walk in the blessings of wisdom, by overcoming personal issues.

Proverbs 2:6   For the Lord giveth wisdom: out of his mouth cometh knowledge and understanding.

Proverbs 3:27   Withhold not good from them to whom it is due, when it is in the power of thine hand to do it.

Correction   You are in control to solve the problems: identify the issues, put in place a plan of action step by step.

Have a meaningful conversation, addressing the problems staying on point.

Note Do not drag up the dead. Concentrate on the now and work on the new.

Self-Examination   Speaking with wisdom, knowledge and understanding using:

Wisdom- analyzes the problem

Knowledge- admit that there is a problem.

Accept Responsibility   Understanding- make an agreement with yourself to change your physical and mental state of mind.

Develop a strategic plan that will force you to stay committed, using strategy allowing for the unexpected.

The plan is strategist because you are serious about changing the progress stoppers, and the blessing blockers.

You will no longer put off today for tomorrow: wasting time and energy, affecting your future.

Proverbs 3:28

Say not unto thy neighbor, Go, and come again, and tomorrow I will give, when thou hast it by thee.

Who is your neighbor: let's start with family first.

Family

Charity starts at home, where your physical, mental, and financial needs are met.

God gives wisdom.
Knowledge is what you know.
Understanding is combining the three together; to improve your life.

Use your knowledge: apply your understanding to the best of your ability. Ask God to give you the strength to follow the leader. (Jesus is the leader)

Window Of Heaven Pouring Out Blessings

Now we understand how blessings operate let us prepare our heart to receive all that God has in store for us.

Remember all roads lead to Jesus even when you cannot see your way. Trust and believe God's word.

The last three chapters illustrate God's blessing operating in people's life under stressful conditions, however when you are committed to the cause of Christ for your sake: follow his instructions and God's plan will give you hope and an great future.

Chapters One- Four

Ruth And Naomi

A book of trust and quiet faith

A great example of windows of heaven pouring our blessings.

Illustrating:
Disappointments
Commitment
Obedience
Patience
Respect
Trust
Virtue/Humility
Favor
Protection
Responsibility

When you read the book of Ruth (only four chapters) you will learn that in the mist of misfortune things do not always turn out as planned.

In this life nothing stays the same, but you must be able to adapt to change.

When you find yourself in a dilemma; should you panic or take time and think things through?

NOTE You cannot predict the future.

Ruth is a great example of a blessing in disguise.

As the plan of God unfolds integrity and obedience rules the day.

Life works on a time frame that requires patience and humility.

Be Ready

When the door of opportunity presents itself step in; remember preparation opens the door.

Position yourself for the blessing, know your purpose.

It is hard to follow a plan to a "T" it requires discipline to make it achievable.

We must learn to follow the procedure that is set before us, do not rush the time frame.

When you are faced with a package deal and forced to decide, weigh all the details.

Through trials and tribulations, the Lord will preserve you and restore your lost.

Joel 2:25

And I will restore to you the years that the locust hath eaten, the cankerworm, and the caterpillar, and the palmerworm, my great army which I sent among you.

Disappointments are part of living however, at the end of the rainbow the sun shines and it is a new day.

Psalm 46:10

Be still, and know that I am God: I will be exalted among the heathen, I will be exalted in the earth.

This book is a guide for all women in retrospect, of self- preservation.

Three short chapters- please read them

Prophet Habakkuk

Across the nation, believers are asking the same question that the prophet Habakkuk ask God.

Why does God permit evil among his people?

The Rich

How can God permit the more wicked to be better off than the righteous?

The necessity of personal faith is the answer, where is your faith?

Time Is Valuable

2020 starts a new decade, a new season and time is on your side if you are alive.

The next ten years moving forward, if God stays his hand, write your vision and make it plain for you and your household.

Self- Preservation

Write your complaints: write truth and honesty standing on the principles of God's word.

Do not worry about the grass that looks so green because when the sun comes out it fades.

Stay Focus

We serve a just God, He is fair. Keep your eyes on the prize because sovereign God the Lord is in control.

Habakkuk 1:5

Behold ye among the heathen, and regard and wonder marvellously: for I will work a work in your days, which ye will not believe, though it be told you.

When you concentrate on the things you cannot control, you lose focus and miss the message that God has for you.

Success does not bring rest, love, peace, satisfaction, or intellectually gratification.

(Sometimes fake security, emptiness, and disgrace).

Starts A New Decade

2020 was the year to eliminate and overcome the normal/common challenges that destroys your vision. They are:

Oops- no remorse.
Excuses- blessing blockers.
Procrastination- progress stoppers.
Tomorrow-is not promised: we do not know what tomorrow will bring or the condition you will be in.
Later- misses the point you lose your thought pattern and sometimes you forget.
Complaints- are distractions: that keep you bound.
Injustice-pollutes society.

Betrayal

Silence- implies tolerance for wrong.
Depression- is an isolated spot: only one person live there why should it be you?
Doubt and fear-captures the day: let the Holy Spirit take control.
Animosity-strong dislike and hatred (hidden) so you think. Not so.

High Expectations

When you understand the plan of God for your life, you realize that God will not tolerate wrong which comes in all shapes and forms.

Perfect Vision For Life Living

When you go to an eye doctor and he says you have 20/20 vision. That is what the word of God gives you.

My First Book

In 2016 the Holy Spirit spoke to my heart to write it down and make it plain incasing personal responsibility and obedience (Memoirs Of a Christian Life)

My soul purpose is to touch your soul, the part that belongs to God.

In Your Mind

When I take you to the mountain top and you peak over and see Zion, when you come down: every day when you wake up you have a chance to work on your plan and see your vision come to pass.

Where do you want to be or anticipate being in ten years from now?

I do not teach or preach hallelujah messages for the moment. God inspired me to write it down and reference the scripture for those that do not read the bible on a daily basis.

Learn to plan and prepare for your future and emergencies by developing a plan that fits your agender.

Coins One Dollar Bills and Etc.

Discipline yourself; start a in house savings account for one year and see what the outcome will be for you and yours (you will like the plan).

Manage your kitchen; groceries are expensive eliminate waste.

When Possible

Practice one trip shopping: grocery store, drug store, dry cleaners etc.

How much can you afford for entertainment without jeopardizing your Plan.

Change bad behavior into good behavior by being responsible for your actions.

A in house savings account is about adjusting in all areas of your life, which comes with patience and sacrifices.

The sole purpose of a vision is to increase insight, promote growth: enabling you to lean on God for strength and direction.

Job's Notebook

A notebook is a book with blank pages; used to keep records and write down information that is useful and important.

Job's notebook; starts with an impeccable reputation.

His mind was saturated with faith in God (positive thinking- I know I can, and I believe he will).
His greatest attributes were perfection: Perfect- no faults
Upright- honest and just
Fear of God- respect
Eschewed evil- avoided wrong

Job 1:1

There was a man in the land of Uz, whose name was Job; and that man was perfect and upright, and one that feared God, and eschewed evil.

His life unraveled with a web of destruction: trusting God for a blessing in disguise.

Allowed

God; initiated (allowed) Satan to excises his power of destruction in Job"s life.

Note: Satan is a limited being who operates within the framework, permitted by God.

God Had Faith In Job

This contest between God and Satan was overruled by faith.

This was a heavy conversation because Satan understood that God had blessed the works of Job's hand and he lived under God's protection.

Job 1:11	"But put forth thine hand now, and touch all that he hath, and he will curse thee to thy face.
Job 1:12	And the Lord said unto Satan, Behold, all that he hath is in thy power; only upon himself put not forth thine hand. So Satan went forth from the presence of the Lord.
Satan	Arrogant and disrespectful, believed his power would supersede God authority.

God Proves A Point

Job 2:2	And the Lord said unto Satan, From whence comest thou? And Satan answered the Lord, and said, From going to and fro in the earth, and from walking up and down in it.
Job 2:3	And the Lord said unto Satan, Hast thou considered my servant Job, that there is none like him in the earth, a perfect and upright man, one that feareth God, and escheweth evil? And still he holdeth fast his integrity, although thou movedst me against him, to destroy him without cause.

Satan attack Job with all of his might, to no avail believing that he would curse God to his face.

God's word is a legal notebook; the law of righteousness which gives you strength to withstand the evils of Satan.

God knows that man's knowledge about his reasoning power is incomplete. It surpasses our understanding; however, we have access to him by faith.

Ultimately God is a hidden mystery, only the believer's who live by faith gains a portion of wisdom and knowledge of his word.

Job Analysis His Condition

Job 1:21
And said, Naked came I out of my mother's womb, and naked shall I return thither: the Lord gave, and the Lord hath taken away; blessed be the name of the Lord.

In this verse (1:21) he answered the messages that brought devastating news.

Frustrated

Job 3:17
There the wicked cease from troubling; and there the weary be at rest.

Trouble Don't Last Always

Job 5:7
Yet man is born unto trouble, as the sparks fly upward.

Job Answers His Critics

Job 13:15
Though he slay me, yet will I trust in him: but I will maintain mine own ways before him.

Job Prayed For Relief

Job 14:14
If a man die, shall he live again? All the days of my appointed time will I wait, till my change come.

Job trusted In His Redeemer

Job 19:25
For I know that my redeemer liveth, and that he shall stand at the latter day upon the earth:

Job Pours Out His Heart

Job 23:10
But he knoweth the way that I take: when he hath tried me, I shall come forth as gold.

The Lord Speaks

Job 37:14

Hearken unto this, O Job: stand still, and consider the wondrous works of God.

Patience

One of the greatest qualities of life is when you can stand still and wait on the Lord.

Restoration

God healed Job's body and restored all of his resource; double fold including his children. Read Job 42: 12-15

When God presides over the case the outcome will always be blessing flowing. He is superior, extraordinary, transcendent and gracious.

The difference in job's notebook and God's legal pad, is authority. He is controlling the universe. God decides how, when, and where, the master has universal authority.

I will go the distance
even when I cannot
see my way

Trust
And
Believe

I will go the distance, even
when I cannot see my way.

Trust
and
Believe

**Trusting And
Believing His Word**

I Will Go The Distance In Jesus Name

You must be committed to go the distance. The journey will not be easy, you will face adversities. Be steadfast in your beliefs.

1 Peter 5:8

Be sober, be vigilant; because your adversary the devil, as a roaring lion, walking about, seeking whom he may devour:

Leaning on God's grace and depending on his mercy.

Grace

Is the goodness of God given to undeserved people?
Grace Covers:
Love- devotion (strong tender feelings)
Favor- kind actions (Helpful)
Honor- great respect (noble deeds)
Dignity- worth (earned respect)
Respect- considerate (showing honor)
Kindness- treatment (kindness is a condition of the heart)

Adorned

In his presence grace brings pleasure and beauty in your life.

Mercy

Is the power to forgive; that's why even the wretch sinners the riff-raff thrives under grace and mercy until they accept Jesus Christ as their Lord and Savior.

Poor And Needy

These are the people that society look down on as being common. (vulgar etc.).

But

God's tender mercy keeps them until the change comes.

Psalms 103:3	Who forgiveth all thine iniquities; who health all thy diseases:
Luke 6:37	Judge not, and ye shall not be judged: condemn not, and ye shall not be condemned: forgive, and ye shall be forgiven:

Man is the instrument used by God to carry out his work with respect, honest, and truth according to his word, as it is written.

God does not give every man the same instruction in the same way, however the instructions he gives is the same word. (uncompromised)

Deuteronomy 4:2	Ye shall not add unto the word which I command you, neither shall ye diminish ought from it, that ye may keep the commandments of the Lord your God which I command you.
Bible	Ministers of the gospel must spend time studying the word of God, asking for wisdom, and understanding of God's word and applying it to themselves first.

Preachers, teachers, prophets, and counselors; if you believe and accept the word of God in its purest form you can help others.

Remember your input affects peoples lives in the natural as well as the spiritual.

2 Timothy 2:15	"Study to shew thyself approved unto God, a workman that needeth not to be ashamed, rightly dividing the word of truth."

There is a penalty for taking matters into your own hands using his word to fit your agenda, your detail planning becomes all about you and yours: remember the storehouse is God's business.

1 Timothy 3:5   (For if a man know not how to rule his own house, how shall he take care of the church of God?)

The Journey   To go the distance your itinerary carries responsibility, from the beginning until the end. The rule of conduct should control your behavior.

As a member of the family of God, know your purpose because once you sign on to right and righteousness, it is a lifetime commitment.

Pray And Fast   Just be willing to carry the load, walking and talking with Jesus believing the end is soon to come according to God's time.

Go back and check your record: while you have a chance. You are never to late to correct your mistakes as long as you are alive and well.

"Revelation"

Jesus Christ; gave John the message and he wrote letters to the church filled with information about the vision of the son of man, and what the tribulation will be like before we can sit around the throne of God; and when it is all over the new heaven and the new earth will appear.

During your travel in time, remember these scriptures:

Revelation 22:18   For I testify unto every man that heareth the words of this prophecy of this book, if any man shall add into these things, God shall add unto him the plagues that are written in this book:

Revelation 22:19

And if any man shall take away from the words of the book of this prophecy, God shall take away his part out of the book of life, and out of the holy city, and from the things which are written in this book.

Song

I'll Go The Distance

Written by   Doris Akers

I heard this song sung at a campmeeting in 2002 with the late (Bishop Eddie Long).

It is heart felt because it addresses the pit falls of life; acknowledging that the road is not easy, but at the end of the tunnel there is light. Just keep the faith.

Second Stanza   I'll go the distance
I will not compromise
Pressing on to win the prize
In Christ Jesus I'll go the distance.

Courage   The race is not given to the swift or the strong, but to the one that endures to the end.

To win the race it takes a made-up mind and a fixed heart to follow Jesus.

Windows Of Heaven Pouring Out Blessings

Memoirs Of A Christian Life Ministry

This book is dedicated to : Memoirs

of a Christian Life Ministry

Founded: October 2018

To receive God's blessings let him

be the center of your life.

When he is in the Center

he pushes all the debris to the side.

Pastor: LTC. Neaice Coleman

Printed in the United States
by Baker & Taylor Publisher Services